WHAT I

An in

Writ

Edite ᴛ ᴋyan

&

Alice O' Byrne

*"I never travel without my diary. One should always
have something sensational to read on the train."*

Oscar Wilde, writer and student at Magdalen
College, Oxford.

Thanks for joining me on another adventure!

This edition published by Alexander Kerr in 2020.

ISBN: 978-1-0867-675-1-4

Printed by Dolman Scott Ltd
www.dolmanscott.co.uk

FOREWORD

I met Alex Kerr in a co-working space when he was just about to finish a chapter for this book about Oxford and we exchanged some ideas about travel publications. His passion and the way he spoke about his hometown, Oxford, made me want to visit that place once again. I'm usually not one that visits the same place twice as the world has so much to offer and there are so many places to see but Alex convinced me to refresh my memories of the academic city north of London and I am convinced you will do the same after putting this book down.

You will also find out in this book that it is very easy to get to Oxford from London, so there are no excuses for not going. I never understood why this is, but it seems that we often neglect the beautiful and exciting places we have on our doorstep and I have made it my mission to inspire people to leave their houses and just explore the world around them. To achieve that, I have launched the blog charlieonthemove.com which tells the adventures of a little monkey, Charlie. It's a blog about travel, people enjoying life, but mostly about experiences in London – where I live – and elsewhere in the world.

When we are going to explore new places - no matter how far away they might be from the place where we live - we will discover beautiful architecture or landscapes, try tasty food, learn new things and meet people. This book about Oxford certainly contains some amazing architecture that inspired many a writer to their stories and you are about to find out about the best places in Oxford for some tasty treats along your journey through this lovely town. Whether you will learn anything new depends on the things you already know but I can say for sure that I learned a lot, not only about the city of Oxford but about

English history and literature whilst reading this book and I am sure you will also discover something you did not know before. Apart from that, be prepared to meet kings and queens, Oscar Wilde and the real person behind the story of Alice in Wonderland (amongst some other exciting personalities).

So, get yourself a cup of tea, find a comfortable spot and let Alex take you on a tour through Oxford. Charlie and I will be by your side, if we are not on another adventure elsewhere.

Julia-Carolin Zeng

(charlieonthemove.com)

PREFACE

"In a world full of fauns, orcs, goblins, wizards and wonders, one tour guide stands alone."

Alex Kerr

I'm from a small town called Abingdon, now Abingdon-on-Thames, and have spent most of my life in 'the city of dreaming spires', Oxford. The Victorian poet, Matthew Arnold, called Oxford 'the city of dreaming spires' in his poem "Thyrsis" after the stunning architecture of the university buildings.

Oxford is a city with so much to see and do and with many hidden gems and history. So, therefore, I thought I'd introduce you to it.

I will say this straight away: I don't think I've ever been in a city, where within 12-20 minutes you can walk from the city centre or other parts such as Cowley or Summertown and find yourself immersed in scenic countryside with few to no people around you. While researching and writing this book, I was stunned by the number of world-class authors who have worked in this city. From Stephen Hawking, who was born here, to Lewis Carrol, C. S. Lewis, Percy Shelly, Oscar Wilde, J. R. R. Tolkien, Colin Dexter and Phillip Pullman, the list is almost ridiculous. There is even evidence that the story of King Arthur was created just outside the city and King Richard the Lion Heart and King John were born here. I do touch on some of the literary characters in this book, but I would rather write a separate one in the future to focus on them.

The outskirts of Oxfordshire also provide plenty of information for a separate book. My aim is to focus on an imagination tour of the city centre. The city centre is full of history and buildings of various ages, and some date to roughly 1000 A.D. with modern ones popping up all the time, including the new shopping centre, the Westgate, an open air mall, which has created a mix of opinions for locals, however, the views from the rooftops are exquisite. The beautiful spires reach higher than any other building and you can see sandstone everywhere.

The older university buildings in the city centre are something to marvel, especially in spring to autumn on sunny days if you can gain access to the colleges. Christ Church, Magdalene College and Brasenose College, as well as many others in the centre, look like something out of a Harry Potter novel, and some scenes from the movies were shot inside those colleges.

The gardens that the colleges own can be spectacular. Flowers from all over the world, which have been sculpted and set in place in such a way that it is calming and inviting to the eye. The gardeners who have tended to these pieces of art are just magnificent.

There is even a deer park in Magdalen College and across the road is Britain's oldest botanical garden, again full of wonders and interesting history. Part of the reason for the gardens and countryside existing is that they are owned by the colleges, and for various reasons, have never had housing.

The botanical garden is not the only first this city has to offer. For example, Oxford offers the first coffee house, first charity shop and the first museum, first telling of King Arthur's legend, and one of the oldest libraries in the world. Unfortunately, on that occasion, Oxford was beaten by the Vatican Library, which was completed in 1475, making it the first in Europe. The oldest continually used library in the world is of al-Qarawiyyin University, Morocco, which opened in 859.

If this does not grab you, there is the castle complex. Once a castle, then a prison and now a shopping and dining centre, with art galleries and hotels with parts of the medieval castle still standing.

If there was a city to visit from London and you only had a weekend in the UK, Oxford is a must. If you are Russian, it seems like a better choice than heading to Salisbury for an hour and heading to a residential area and a gas station instead of visiting Stonehenge and Salisbury cathedral.

Today, I'm going to give you the first step in a tour of Oxford.

CONTENTS

GETTING TO, AND AROUND, OXFORD

Getting to Oxford from London could not be easier. Oxford is located 56 miles north-west of London. It is 400 miles south of Scotland and 180 miles east of Wales. It is an area further from the coast than any other city in the country. The city is spoilt with direct buses from the airports, and London city centre has trains from Paddington as well as buses from various locations to the west of central London.

By Bus

The Oxford Tube is a super convenient and cheap service that'll take you from the centre of London straight into the heart of Oxford. If you're taking this route, I'd recommend getting off at the High Street so that you can begin your tour at Magdalen College.

There was an X90, but this will close on January 2020. From Heathrow, you can get the National Express.

By Car
Oxford is only an hour/hour and a half drive from the centre of London. It's a very easy drive down via the M4, M25, M40 and A roads. Be warned: It is best not to bring your car into the town, as there is limited parking and it is frankly a bit of a maze. Even Jeremy Clarkson, *Top Gear* host and Oxfordshire resident, struggled with the layout of the town.

By Train
There are regular trains from London Paddington to Oxford. The station is a little way out of the city centre, but you can take a bus or walk into town. The buses are in front of the station and you need to look for the city buses, such as the city 5, city X3, city X13, or city 13, which will take you into the city centre. If you are really stuck, there are taxis.

By Foot and Bike

These are the best ways of getting around the town centre. If you are not used to cycling in a busy city, it might be best to walk instead.

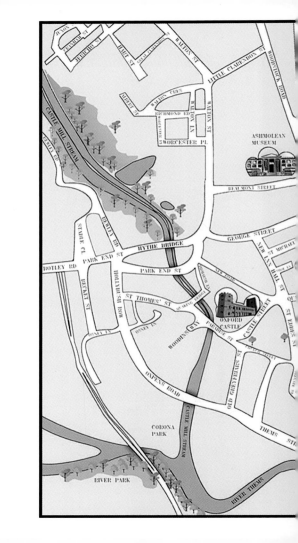

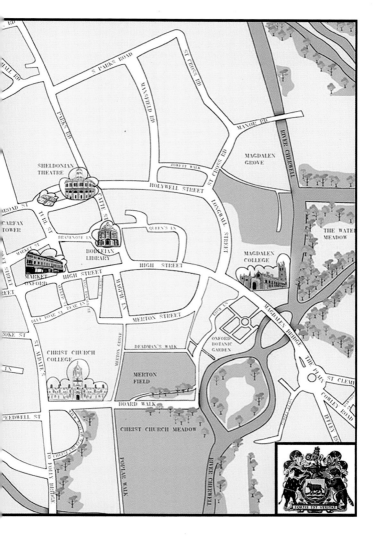

Chapter One

THE BEGINNING OF YOUR IMAGINATION TOUR

Magdalen College

Colin Dexter, the writer of *Inspector Morse*, said:

"The huge value for me as a writer is that, even if people haven't been to Oxford, they would love to be in the city."

Imagine you got off the bus from London at Oxford High Street. We begin our imaginary tour through this magnificent city at Magdalen College. We are starting the tour from Magdalen Bridge and will be going through the city centre.

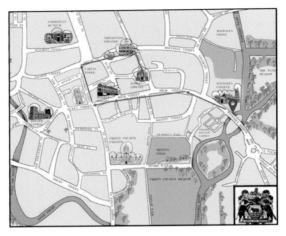

This is something very different, as most of you would probably be used to this on a YouTube format, but here we are going to have to use our imagination.

Magdalen Bridge is beautiful and links the city centre to a lovely area of Oxford called Cowley.

The bridge, in my opinion, is quite romantic, wide with old gas lights converted to electric, and sand-coloured stone walls set on either side.

There has been a bridge on this spot for over a thousand years. The current one is a few hundred years old. It did have a tradition with Oxford University students- with these bright minds throwing themselves off the bridge. However, after several years of students throwing themselves off the bridge and then being taken to the John Radcliffe Hospital, the local council now have police shut off the bridge during the 1st of May celebrations. The date holds significance to many different cultures that have inhabited Britain. The Celts, the Romans, and the modern British, all have celebrated this date. There are normally celebrations relating to fertility, spring and summer.

During May 1st, certain rules are allowed in the city such as all-night drinking in pubs, bars and the college bars throughout Oxford, which is a rarity for the city (yes, the colleges of the universities have bars, and some have cafés. Magdalen College has a café by the bridge overlooking the River Cherwell).

The tradition goes, students would stay up all night with the aim of listening to a choir that would sing in the early morning of May 1st from inside the college's tower and get into punt boats located at a quay at the bottom of the bridge. A punt is a boat that may contain oars but also a long stick or pole. A person stands at the back of the boat and drives the pole into the bottom of the river to propel you forward. You can still access or hire this today. Unfortunately, due to people being drunk, several boats were damaged, so, the practice was stopped. The logical conclusion was for these students to throw themselves off the bridge. In the end, to stop our young bright minds from damaging themselves due to the river being shallow, police are now brought in to block the bridge and stop people throwing themselves in. You can still hear the singing from the choir at

Magdalen College Tower, which is quite a beautiful thing to be heard after a long night of drinking. The tower was built in the 1400s and is a beautiful feature of the Oxford landscape that helps make Oxford 'the city of dreaming spires.'

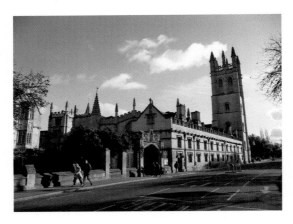

As our tour leaves the bridge, we have two very interesting buildings on either side. Magdalen College, with quite a bit of history, and the botanical gardens opposite.

The college is stunning and, I assume, had a part to play in inspiring J. K. Rowling. You enter to the right of the street. There is a small entry fee and you are spoilt by Gothic, Grecian and medieval-styled buildings and wonderful gardens.

As you enter, you come into a courtyard. To your left are the old grammar hall and student rooms. To the right you will see a small entrance into the cloisters, a door on the right of this entrance takes you into the chapel. Even if you are not religious it is worth entering to see the beautiful stained-glass windows. There is also a tapestry of da Vinci's Last Supper, which will allow you to debate over the person to the right of Jesus being male or female.

As you leave, head right, and you'll come into a cloister, made extra famous by *Harry Potter*, and further on you will see an entrance to the garden and grass in the centre. To my knowledge, you cannot set foot on this grass until you have finished your exams at the university. To the right is the dining hall, again straight out of a Harry Potter story, but also where students go to dine three times a day if they care to spend their money that way. Two interesting busts sit on opposite sides of the hall. To the right, Oscar Wilde, and to the left is supposedly the judge that sent him to jail for being gay. It is not, but that is for another book.

You may visit Wilde's room or even rent it out. The college allows people to do their own tour of the grounds and to stay within the college during the holidays.

Many famous people have attended the college. Two of note were C.S. Lewis, the writer of *Narnia,* and Howard Florey, the inventor/discoverer of penicillin.

I will bring up C.S. Lewis on another occasion. Florey has an interesting tale of his own.

During his days at Oxford during World War II he carried out trials of penicillin at John Radcliffe Hospital. His first patient was a policeman who had pricked his finger on a rose and had acquired an infection. Florey administered the penicillin and though the officer initially recovered, there was not enough penicillin being produced and the officer died.

During this period, they had discovered that bedpans were a useful device for producing penicillin. Due to there being a shortage of everything during World War II, they scoured the local dumps to gain any spare bedpans. Unfortunately, and fortunately, Florey couldn't get the U.K. government interested in the project and left the UK to the USA to produce more penicillin. By 1945, the drug was mass-produced and has gone on to save millions of lives.

Back to our tour through the college. As you go down from the steps and into cloisters, to the right you will see the bar and café. Pictures of celebrities and oars from successful races cover the walls. The cafe contains one more gem: an outside seating area for drinks and food, which gives you views of the gardens and the River Cherwell where you can see people punting away down the river.

Out of the café and on with the walk, onto the gravel path, into the gardens, and to the deer park. Yes, the college contains a deer park known as the Grove.

Over the small college bridge and into the park itself. The deer are fenced in but you can almost always see them. The area had originally consisted of orchards, games areas and it housed Royalist troops during the English Civil War, (1642–1651).

Many rumours abound with these deer. During World War II the deer were supposedly classified as vegetables to save them from rationing. There are also claims that when a dean of the college dies or retires they kill and eat a deer as part of the celebrations of service. I am yet to see proof of this.

That is the first step in this tour of Oxford, much more to come.

Chapter Two

BOTANICAL GARDENS

Oxford still remains the most beautiful thing in England, and nowhere else are life and art so exquisitely blended, so perfectly made one. Oscar Wilde

We move away from Magdalen Bridge and Magdalen College, and across the road to the botanical gardens. These are the oldest botanical gardens in the UK and the oldest scientific gardens in the world.

It is open from 10-5 pm, (last entry is at 4:15) and tickets are £5-6.

The entrance is opposite the college and resembles a typical Roman triumphant monument: It's known as the Danby Gateway, which is fair enough as the garden is a triumph.

The grounds are over 4.5 acres, and contain over 8000 species of plants.

It has an interesting history as it was once a Jewish cemetery until the Jews were kicked out of the country in 1290. The area was then used for the city's waste, a dumping point, which has today provided the area with lush fertile soil. However, an extra 4000 cartloads of manure were needed in the 1600s to raise the area above the flood plain, thus allowing it to become the garden it is today. The garden even produces its own alcohol from its plants, including a superb gin, in very limited amounts. As you can imagine, with the array of plants and excellent fertile soils the alcohols are expensive but well worth it.

The garden has inspired at least three Oxford literary geniuses: Philip Pullman, Charles Dodgson and J.R.R. Tolkien. In the final chapter of *His Dark Materials* by Philip Pullman, you note that Will and Lyra talk of sitting on a bench at noon on every Midsummer's Day. You can find the bench William and Lyra sat on, with plenty of graffiti for their love. We believe that Dodgson of *Alice in Wonderland* frequently took Alice Liddell and her sisters to the garden. The garden features in the drawing in *Alice in Wonderland's* the "The Queen's Croquet-Ground." We also believe that a tree that inspired Treebeard from *The Lord of The Rings* was in the gardens, a *Pinus nigra*. Unfortunately, the tree had to be cut down in 2014. The black pine tree had been planted in 1799 and was a favourite of Tolkien's. The tree lost two of its limbs and therefore had to be gotten rid of.

As we move past the botanical gardens we start to into the city and along High Street.

Chapter Three

THE HIGH STREET

On the left is the exam hall, an interesting part of Oxford University life. As we go down Merton Street, you will come across some magnificent buildings, including the original grand entrance to the exam hall. The current main entrance appears to be on the High Street; a large courtyard made of a beautiful sandstone colour.

Although I didn't go to the university, I had many friends there and dated someone who studied there. The university appears to create an interesting social situation with the colleges. The students are encouraged and tested for three years. Many students are within the college accommodation for three years. At the end of the three years, the students take their final exams for their university qualifications.

Having been inside the colleges for three years, having high levels of academic training and lectures, plus being around students who are generally academically competitive and confident, the students become increasingly stressed and study focused. I bore witness to students sleeping all night inside the libraries, to then rise and study once more. I knew ladies who were pulling their hair out, to such an extent that in their third year they were creating bald patches. When speaking to their doctor, they were told not to worry as this was "normal" and should stop after the exams. Of course, there were more carefree students but the general note was extreme stress. From a student perspective, if "Tom or Jane" were studying then I had to do the same. Being in such a closed environment, everyone pretty much knew what everyone else was doing all the time.

There are some interesting rumours surrounding the exams themselves. One involves turning up in a full suit of armour, on a white horse, and your reward is receiving a glass of sherry or potentially a first in your degree. Whilst I was a student, there is even rumour of someone having done this in recent years. The college had countered this by stating that no weapons were permitted on the grounds and thus a full suit of armour could not be worn inside the exam hall.

The other exam tradition involves bringing in old English money, known as a shilling, and if you can find and bring 2 shillings to the exam you apparently can order a flagon/ pint of ale. As stated, these are only rumours but there is a book with all the exam rules, known as 'the Doorstop'. I assume the name reflects the size and not the usage.

Upon finishing the exams, students exit the back of the exam halls onto the cobbled part of Merton street, with the road leading to Merton College and Christ Church. Entrance is free around June and July. Students pile out of the exam hall, to be met by friends who proceed to cover them in glitter, alcohol and if they are lucky, milk that has been left by a radiator for a month. These are the joys of getting legitimate revenge on someone you've lived with for three years.

Chapter Four

THE HIGH STREET

As we move along the widening streets of Oxford and into the heart of the city centre, we pass two of Britain's oldest coffee shops. Both offer a curious look into the past.

Established in the UK around 1650–1652, the coffee shop was something originally open to all with a penny entry fee. With this would come the coffee and access to newspapers, pamphlets, and debates. The curious thing is why this didn't continue and why it has only just resurfaced with chain stores producing drinks that are nothing particularly special in taste, and a cappuccino costing something in the region of £5. It seems crazy that people would go there instead of these two old Oxford cafés. In Sicily, a cappuccino is £1.50, and if you were to try it, it would probably convert you into not attending the coffee chains. Pretty much all coffee comes from either South America or Vietnam, so it does make you wonder what is happening to inflate UK chain store costs, for coffee of lower quality and more sugar.

The apparent reason for coffee shops disappearing was elitism. Certain groups in society did not want people they considered to be commoners entering the shops, which drove down business, pushed people to the pubs and eventually caused a culture shift in coffee drinking.

The two coffee shops I would like to visit with you have different claims. The Grand Cafe claims to be the first coffee shop in the UK, and I believe they claim to have the biggest one-piece mirror in Europe.

Queens Lane Coffee Shop claims to be the longest continuous coffee shop in Europe. A claim I know is being fought for in Venice and Milan, both having cafés with equal and longer claims.

Chapter Five

ALL SOULS COLLEGE

ontinuing along the sand-coloured stone buildings and colleges, we come to a college called All Souls. It was attended by Christopher Wren, who features in this book regularly as well as Robert Recorde, the man who created the equal (=) sign in 1557.

All Souls is a curious college, with no undergraduates. Students may apply upon completion of their exams. They then take an exam, once considered to be one of the "hardest exams in the world." A friend of mine took the test, or at least claims to have. He said that the test consisted of a single word. I believe it was the word "cow" and then he was expected to write a full essay based on this one word. What he wrote I cannot remember, but interesting, nonetheless. After the exam, those selected will be asked to attend an interview. If you pass this, you are given accommodation for a year in the college, you become a fellow of the college, and you receive money to help support your studies. It has also been claimed that you may take the accommodation and money but you do not have to work. Interesting bonus for the year if you decide to take the exam. The college has years of not taking students and if they do, it is normally only one student.

Finally, to add to the wackiness, there is a centenary tradition around January. On the first year of each new century (2001) fellows have dinner and then go in search of a duck to kill (a wooden one as of 2001). The rumour goes that a duck was found in the brickwork during the construction of the college, although I've also heard that this was a dream. Either way, I'm sure conspiracy theorists will come to their own conclusions with this strange ritual.

Chapter Six

UNIVERSITY COLLEGE

To our left is the University College. It's had several Prime Ministers, Australian and British, American President Clinton, Steven Hawking and a current member of the US Supreme Court. One of the most interesting characters at the college was Prince Yusupov, the man who killed Grigori Rasputin.

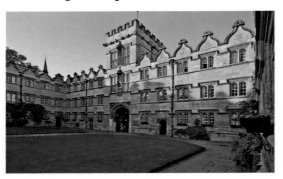

Rasputin was a Russian from Siberia, born in 1869 into the lower Russian classes. He rose to prominence by religious conversion and the apparent ability to heal the sick, with some extraordinary accounts coming from doctors, army officers and members of the aristocracy. The accounts are both credible and incredible. The king (also known as Tsar, supposedly from the word Caesar) had a son who suffered from haemophilia. No cure was known at the time, other than rest. If you were cut, bruised or any form of bleeding occurred, it was difficult for your body to heal it. Several incidents happened that caused the royal family to call on Rasputin's abilities to come to heal the boy.

I've seen accounts from doctors who claimed that he just waved his hand over the child and the bleeding stopped. One conclusion is that his words would calm the child, allowing him to rest, but even today doctors are baffled by this. Nonetheless, Rasputin gained favour in the courts. The Tsar and Tsarina ignored his behaviours such as orgies and drinking. Rasputin could link religion and sin through repenting. The idea was that even though they are a sin, you could repent, making yourself pure again or even purer. It might have been accepted because a large number of people would nullify the effects. They all would instantly absolve each other. He was accused of seducing women of the court, married and single. There are even rumours of an affair with the Tsarina. Due to his influence in court, he sold government positions in exchange for money or favours.

Considering this was the age of kings/tsars and tsarinas/queens and social mobility was not possible for most, Rasputin climbed the social hierarchy quickly and to its greatest heights. During the war, he was even given authority over military matters.

This was to come to an end in 1916, when Felix Yusupov lead the move to assassinate

Rasputin. Rasputin came to Yusupov's estate. He took food and drink laced with cyanide, but it had no effect. Yusupov, shocked by this, went upstairs and shot him. Believing he was dead, Yusupov and the other conspirators took off in a car. They returned to Rasputin's home, to make it look as if Rasputin had returned home. When Yusupov came back to check on the body, Rasputin jumped to his feet and attacked Yusupov before attempting to flee. Yusupov and his conspirators wrapped the body in a carpet and threw it off a nearby bridge.

Rasputin had prophesied that if he died, Russia would lose the war and the government/monarchy would collapse. He died in December and the tsar abdicated in March the following year. Felix and his wife moved out of Russia, near to Sicily on the island of Malta, and settled in France. Felix wrote an account of the death of Rasputin in the 1920s and died in the 1960s.

Chapter Seven

BRASENOSE COLLEGE

*"The only thing necessary for the triumph of evil is
for good men to do nothing."*

Edmund Burke

As we reach closer to the centre and see the Carfax Tower, we walk past Brasenose College. This college has some sinister and strange traditions that are now becoming the norm as we continue our trip through Oxford.

Brasenose College, which has the name supposedly due to the brass knocker at its front gate, has a reputation for being connected to the Hellfire Club through another sinister tale. Several witnesses claim to have seen a student being dragged through the tiny and barred windows of a college room.

On a cold, winter's day in December 1872, a meeting of the Hellfire Club was taking place, when one of its members was dragged to Hell, supposedly by the Devil. According to accounts, this was witnessed by members of the college and an employee. Also, witnesses outside the college testify that they saw a man in a long cloak outside this student's room.

This supposedly occurred because the student was notorious for being bad. You might not think much of this, yet we do hear strange rumours rearing its ugly pig's head even today. Other members of this college include the inventor of rugby football, William Webb Ellis, an Archbishop, a Prime Minister of Australia and a Python (Monty kind). I am trying not to make the college and alumni sound sinister. Promise.

From these tales of terror, we move to the centre of the city and Carfax Tower (St Martin's Church), which has an interesting and important tale for the city. The tower is what remains of a church from the 12th century. The tower sets two rules (bylaws) for the city and its students. No university students can live a certain number of miles from the tower and no building in the city can be built higher than this tower, which means roughly four storeys or 73/74 feet in height. The partial reason for this is to protect the architecture of the Oxford buildings. Even Hitler, the nasty piece of work that he was, recognised that this city was not to be bombed due to him wanting to keep the architecture intact, according to documents taken from Berlin on Operation Sea Lion (the invasion of Britain by Germany), which contained detailed information on Oxford and the bridge at Abingdon with the aim of turning the city of Oxford into his capital. These documents and a recently written book on the invasion plan can be found in the Bodleian Library. However, the current city council in its wisdom has decided to debate whether to keep this up (you can tell a campaign is brewing here).

The city has been known for decades and centuries for its beautiful sandstone buildings, with classical architecture, and 'dreaming spires.' You can see these by walking to the top of several buildings including the Carfax Tower, St. Mary's Church and the Westgate Shopping Mall. The law is obviously there to protect these views and buildings, which help give Oxford a unique feel. Yet the council seem oblivious to this, or uncaring, only hoping to build tall high-rise buildings, probably to help its tax income by having more people in the town. The issue with this is that it helps to continue the trend of making cities look generic, exemplified by the way they made the new shopping mall (that I will save for a later rant).

They have even put forward plans for a new tower to be installed in Cornmarket Street, which until the new Westgate Shopping Mall was built was one of the main streets of the city. Again, this is something we will discuss more later. Many members of the public denounced this as it was not in keeping with the views. The real kicker was when a spokeswoman came out to defend the design. The key point used was that it would allow the board of directors in charge of the project to have a good view of Cornmarket during board meetings in the tower. We seem to be continuing a trend of *"We have money, we are building this, and we couldn't care less about what others think as we are getting a great view."* It feels like a sinister scene out of an episode of *The Simpsons*, with Mr Burns. I can picture the boardroom, with his hellfire chair, triple the size of any other chair, with demons coming out of the back and two fierce guard dogs chained to the side, as he looks out onto the town of dreaming spires, citing his famous line of, "Excellent. How long till the trap door is built?"

I demonise, but with justice, as there are other parts of the city that could do with development, with investment and support that would not damage the view, yet no word is spoken of these areas, as the city centre seems to continually be the focus point. In a recent bit of reading, I discovered that Bill Bryson almost word for word repeated what I had said about the city centre. The ideas of modern architects coming in and shaking up the place, trying something new and, but for a few exceptions, failing. They force this modern view of how the buildings should look and ignore the people who must look at their creations.

Not all parts of Oxford's stories can be full of promise and delight; the unfortunate realities of the world, but you now have a taste of how a city council works.

Chapter Eight

OXFORD VS CAMBRIDGE

I am a tour guide of this city and its history and have been giving tours for almost a decade. Whenever I give a tour of Oxford, one of the first things I get asked is, "How was the Oxford and Cambridge rivalry created?"' As we continue our tour, if you are facing the Carfax Tower, to your left you will see a bank, which used to be a tavern and links to the foundation of Cambridge.

The story has varying accounts but what we believe to be true is that the university split had its beginnings in 1209 when locals hanged two students for the murder of a young woman. Students left the town and some moved to Cambridge. The town was already known for its scholarly research and this helped Cambridge University to grow.

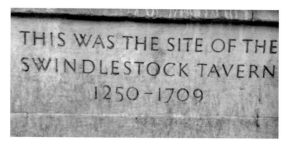

THIS WAS THE SITE OF THE
SWINDLESTOCK TAVERN
1250 - 1709

Many people feel that the creation of the university was in 1355. This is not the case. There was more bloodshed with the town and students, caused by an argument in the Swindlestock tavern.

Although a bank has taken over the tavern, there is a memorial stone that sits in its place.

The argument seems to have started over a drink; two students complained about some wine they had been sold. The barman gave a snappy response, and the students, in turn, poured the wine over the barman and a bar brawl broke out.

The next day, the two students were requested to meet with the bailiffs and the Mayor, but they refused. The head of the university, the Chancellor, was asked to intervene but refused. Instead, the bell of St. Mary's church was rung and roughly 200 students came into the streets and proceeded to fight the Mayor and his associates. This caused the local townspeople to join in. Instead of resolving the conflict, the fighting only grew as people from the surrounding countryside started to come into the town to join the fight. This caused riots, which led to an estimated 90 deaths and some scapings.

Eventually, King Edward III was brought into the situation. He happened to be 8 miles away in a town called Woodstock. The King had been born there and as a result, spent periods of the year in the town and this coincided with the riots.

(Interesting fact: Elizabeth the 1st would also spend time in this town as a prisoner and it is home to Blenheim Palace, where Winston Churchill was born.)

Once the rioting died down, the King requested that judges investigate the matter. Blame was placed on the townspeople, and the university was given further powers to control the town's running, food and upkeep.

Furthermore, an annual custom was created. On February 10th, a mass would be held with the mayor and councillors, where they would pay 1 penny for each person killed. To give you an idea of value, 1 penny could feed a person for a day at that time.

This lasted until 1825 when the then Mayor of Oxford simply refused to attend, ending the tradition and punishment—almost 500 years after the event!

Chapter Nine

CORNMARKET STREET

We are at a crossroad of where to go next. This is what the word Carfax means in old French, 'four ways.' Carfax Tower in front, the new mall behind, and the castle beyond that. Right takes us to Cornmarket, which was the main street for shopping until the new mall opened.

To the left is Christ Church. So many choices, and thankfully so much time. To the right is Cornmarket again with an interesting history. We will come back to the castle and Christ Church later in the book. Don't get too comfortable. It doesn't stand out and, to be honest, I think they could have something quite beautiful here. The street is wide and pedestrianised, yet totally open to the elements. There are no covered walkways, no cafés in the street, nor a fountain for when England win the World Cup (It is a tradition to celebrate great national victories in London by jumping into the fountains in Trafalgar Square, so why not start a tradition here?) Ok, a point of fantasy about the fountain, but there is something horribly remarkable about this street, hidden in plain sight: The benches. When you make it to Cornmarket Street, take your time to walk along and count the number of benches. Whilst doing this, try to guess how much you think the city council spent on these benches. We will come back to this later.

Supposedly, every shop to the right up to St Michael's Tower is owned by one of the university colleges. Rumour has it that the entire right-hand side is owned by Jesus College. There is some evidence to support this: a new building has been proposed this year (2019) and it is being built by Jesus College for the cheap price of £36 million.

As we make it halfway down, to the left is a small alley with arguably one of the most underrated underground clubs in Oxford and the Oxford University Union, which is still open. However, as of writing this, the Cellar has now shut down. It was notorious. It hosted a wide array of hip hop and drum and bass artists, as well as some comedy legends, such as Stewart Lee, both the Holly's from the TV show *Red Dwarf*, Russell Howard and it is where Jack Whitehall started his career as a compere for a full season. Above ground is the Oxford Union, which contains a lovely subsidised bar and has hosted debates with famous people from all over the world, including Winston Churchill, the Dalai Lama, Albert Einstein, Stephen Hawking and Malcolm X. You can even see some of these debates on YouTube. You can become a member and attend debates through the Oxford Union website, as either a resident or if you have studied at the university. As an Oxford resident, you will need to meet with officers of the Union to be allowed in.

To your right, we come to the supposedly oldest building in Oxford: A Saxon Tower, almost 1000 years in age and attached to St Michael's church.

The Tower has an infamous history, with part of its history being tied to a prison, which is for a later story and a curious tale involving King Edward II and a cat.

John Powderman was living in Oxford in the 1300s when he decided to enter the royal residence in Beaumont Street and claimed to be King Edward II himself. He was tall and good-looking but there was one problem. When queried about his claim, they asked why he had lost an ear. He claimed that a nurse had let him be attacked by a pig whilst playing in the courtyard. Knowing she would be severely punished, she swapped the child. He then claimed this was why Edward had such strange habits and that he would challenge him in one to one combat for the throne. Eventually, he was arrested and met the King. Powderman, not short on courage, insulted the King and offered trial by combat. Instead, the King put him on trial, where Powderman confessed it was a lie and that whilst walking through Christchurch Meadow a cat had convinced him to tell this lie. He and the cat were hanged!

We are now coming to the end of Cornmarket Street. How many benches did you count?

Take that number and divide it by the figure of £250,000. Reported by the Oxford Mail in April 2004, the apparent reason for a quarter of a million being spent was that local officials blamed each other for the spiralling costs, and no one would take responsibility. Of course, the bench makers in the background are rubbing their hands with glee. The worse thing about these benches is that they are designed to be comfortable for only a short period of time. One side has curved seats like that of a banana. The other side has seats that would make a Ryanair seat look elegant and feel comfortable.

When these benches were built, they thought of visitors with reduced mobility. How nice of them to leave a clear space next to a delightful bin, with the opening to the bin at roughly head height to someone sitting in a wheelchair. The reason for this design is to get people to not sit for too long so they go to the next shop, to stop anti-social behaviour and to stop homeless people from sitting or sleeping on them at night. There are an estimated 100 to 150 homeless people in Oxford according to various sources, including the local homeless shelter, the *Guardian* newspaper and the city council. Considering the almighty cost, the council could have just turned this around by buying some classic wooden benches. I've found a fountain for £3000 with installation included.

Some wooden benches for roughly £300 and the rest of the money totalling £243,000 could have gone to the homeless shelter and food banks. Just an idea, for helping and not deliberately hindering others who are already suffering and in need of support.

Chapter Ten

BROAD STREET

Once again, we are at a crossroads and its decision time. There are two options to go straight ahead to St Giles, and Beaumont Street, which contains a famous museum, a celebrated pub and a not-so-renowned street, or to turn right onto Broad Street and learn about one of the UK's largest libraries, the location of the oldest museum and hear some great practical jokes... To the right and Broad Street, it is! We will come back to the museum and other locations later in the book.

Broad Street plays itself as a strange contrast: broad in name and size and crammed with so much information I was almost daunted by the task of writing about it.

As you come onto the street, to your left are two colleges, Balliol and Trinity, with sandy coloured stone, and beautiful gardens, which are well worth a visit.

Whilst the college buildings themselves would not look out of place in a *Harry Potter* book, to your right, you have multicoloured shops, light pink and blue that are somehow not out of place and are full of history.

The shops are the site of the old castle wall, which was eventually torn down, but if you go behind 6 Broad Street there is still an old bastion from the wall. On the same side is the very first charity shop, Oxfam, marked with a classic blue plaque. This opened in 1942. If you're not too careful you might miss in the middle of Broad Street, opposite the Fudge Factory Shop, a cross made out of cobbled stones.

The cross marks the location where Protestants were burnt during the reign of Mary I. Her father was Henry the VIII, he died in 1547, and he had left the Catholic Church and created a Protestant religion making himself Head of the English Church. There are some very interesting parallels to Brexit here. He separated from the Church in Rome, the Catholic Courts and effectively Europe. This had split the country in half with the population either wanting to be Catholic or Protestant. When Henry VIII died in 1547, he left a Protestant son Edward the VI and he died in 1553. Edward left the crown to his Protestant cousin Lady Jane Grey. She was a very short-lived Queen and only lasted for 9 days. Henry VIII's eldest daughter, Mary Tudor, also known as Mary I or Bloody Mary was Catholic, and she took the throne from Lady Jane Grey. During her reign, she burnt 280 Protestants and several of those were killed in Oxford, including the Archbishop of Canterbury. They say on misty mornings in summer you can smell the burning of the townspeople.

Colleges on Broad Street

Balliol (1263) and Trinity (1555) on our left are two old, rich and established colleges. 7 prime ministers, 5 noble laureates, a big bumbling Boris; the new Prime Minister, and a Dawkins talking about an evolution tree. As you may tell, at the time of writing this was around Christmas and couldn't resist a stab at a Christmas carol.

There is quite a rivalry between the colleges, with plenty of pranks. The best I heard was students from Trinity sending letters with glass containers to new students at Balliol. The letter stated that medical tests were required and that they were to give the urine samples to their tutors by no later than 5 pm Wednesday. 57 were returned. This culminated in the Trinity pranksters unfurling a banner in Balliol say, "We are Balliol. Please don't take the piss."

Back to Broad Street

As we continue, the street widens. During Christmas, there are fantastic weekend markets with local or regionally produced food. Supposedly underneath our feet lies a room of the Bodleian Library that is for student research and reading. The Bodleian Library is a book depository system. Supposedly every book that is published worldwide is meant to be sent to the library where it is catalogued and made ready for students to access. I've had friends who have claimed there are tunnels under the city, filled with books, that stretch for miles and that to get around some of these tunnels you are given a bike and sent in a direction to collect. I'm even aware of a friend being given access to the library, where he discovered a piece of poetry by Keates. We will come back to the Bodleian in chapter eleven.

The street was the original outer part of the city, which was not only known for burning and hanging people but also selling horses. The original name of the street was horse mongers, and that is where the White Horse pub on the left, in part, gets its name.

The White Horse is also linked to the area due to the white horse being linked to the Vale of the White Horse; an area of government administration that is linked to the famous White Horse in Uffington.

On the opposite side of the pub is the oldest
museum in Europe, (1638) if not the world.
It is now known as the Science Museum and
contains many items dating back to antiquity,
but one item stands out for me is Einstein's
blackboard. He escaped persecution in
Germany and was offered a place in Oxford,
where he lectured. After one of these lectures,
some tutors removed the blackboard that he
had written on and it is now located inside
the Science Museum.

The Science Museum was the original
location of the Ashmolean Museum, which
moved in 1894 to its current location on
Beaumont Street, a much larger building
near the crossroads at the beginning of Broad
Street. We will also visit the museums in
chapter 13.

As you move back into the street, there is the
Sheldonian Theatre designed by Christopher
Wren, a famous architect from Britain who

attended and lectured at Oxford University. He designed 52 churches, including St Paul's in London, the Royal Observatory and the Sheldonian Theatre in Oxford. This theatre has had a fascinating start but also reached a peak when it became England's Parliament, albeit for a week during the 1640s.

King Charles I was not having the best of times with Parliament. He needed money for war and Parliament would not give it to him. He closed it between 1628 to 1640, a total of 11 years, making him very unpopular. When fighting between England and Scotland started, he recalled Parliament asking for more money for an army. They again refused and he closed parliament. Parliament began to build an army, as did the King, and the two sides went to war. In May 1644, he left London and moved to Oxford, which was considered a royalist centre. He established the Sheldonian as his Parliament.

The rest of the tale of King Charles I will come later. However, if you leave the Sheldonian and cross the road, you will see Blackwell's Bookshop, and as you go inside, it quickly becomes apparent this building is a bit of a Tardis. As you go downstairs you will see pictures on the wall showing the history of Oxford, including some dogs dressed as soldiers. There are some that are King Charles' Spaniels, linking it to the English Civil War. As you go into the basement, it opens into a huge room, supposedly in the Guinness Book of Records for being the largest room with books to be sold. If stacked together in a line, they would reach 3 miles in length.

Chapter Eleven

ᴛHE BODLEIAN LIBRARY

"There are few greater temptations on earth than to stay permanently at Oxford in meditation, and to read all the books in the Bodleian."

Oscar Wilde

We head towards the end of our journey and walk past the Sheldonian Theatre, through the Bodleian and onto the Radcliffe Camera and St Mary's Church.

The Bodleian Library, as mentioned in the previous chapter, is a gigantic library in the heart of Oxford city centre. To get access to the university's books, anyone can join, but it is easier if you are at either of the Oxford universities.

As we come from Broad Street, we can go up some steps, through to a courtyard containing the Sheldonian Theatre, from where you can see a covered bridge linking two college buildings.

Opposite is Hertford Bridge, also known as the Bridge of Sighs. There is a myth that it was constructed to reflect a bridge in Venice where prisoners were taken to their cells and they would cross the bridge and sigh  at the beautiful and possibly final sight of Venice. Hence the name, Bridge of Sighs. I personally think it looks nothing like the aforementioned bridge and more like another bridge in Venice called the Rialto Bridge. Nevertheless, the Hertford Bridge does look beautiful and can be fun on drunken nights. If you stand underneath you can hear a clear echo.

If you turn right when facing the bridge from the courtyard, you can enter a passage built by Christopher Wren, which takes you into a smaller square courtyard.

Before you go in, to the left if facing the Bridge of Sighs, you will see the old University Press building. When facing the entrance, you can see to the far right of the building indented back—these are the exam rooms that were used in *Harry Potter* as the infirmary.

Go through the entrance and you enter the quad of the Bodleian. It resembles something out of *Harry Potter*, with elaborate designs of sand-coloured stone, a clock tower to your left, and a lifelike statue of the Earl of Pembroke, almost standing guard over the library and building. He was Chancellor of the University, founded Pembroke College, and Shakespeare dedicated his first folio to him. Not too shabby for a life's work. Shakespeare was meant to have visited Oxford and the Crown Pub on Cornmarket claims to have been his local haunt.

If you continue through the quad and exit on the other side, you come out onto cobbled streets (cobbled streets are very good for working the glutes) and you are confronted with the Radcliffe Camera in Radcliffe Square. A unique round building in the centre of town, which is where you can go to collect your books from the Bodleian Library. Iron railings, with bicycles chained to it, surround the building, and an oval-shaped grass lawn separates the railings and camera (Camera is Latin for Chamber is Cameras are associated with being reading rooms), creating a very quintessential Oxford University feel to the square. To the left, you can see All Souls College and to the right Brasenose College.

The Bodleian Library is supposed to have a copy of every book printed. Some of its more ancient pieces include:

1. A copy of the Magna Carta
2. Shakespeare's first folio (book of his plays and poetry)
3. The Gutenberg Bible (one of the earliest mass-printed Bibles)

If you want to look at these books you can only do so inside the library. There, you must make an oath, either written or said aloud:

"I hereby undertake not to remove from the Library, nor to mark, deface, or injure in any way, any volume, document or other object belonging to it or in its custody; not to bring into the Library, or kindle therein, any fire or flame, and not to smoke in the Library; and I promise to obey all rules of the Library."

The Radcliffe Camera

The Radcliffe Camera was completed in 1749 and is probably one of the most famous buildings in Oxford. It's linked to Tolkien and

claimed to be the basis of one of the great castles led by the side of Evil in the *Lord of the Rings*. Personally, I can't see a resemblance; it's just too beautiful to be evil.

As we work our butts off walking the cobbled streets, we come to St Mary's Church next to the Radcliffe Camera. The church has existed on this site for almost 1000 years. It saw the Oxford martyrs tried inside and the scene of the Oxford Graduations ceremony until the 1600s. The main thing to really take note of is climbing the church's spiral staircase to the top. Recently redesigned, it now includes a giant map of Oxford to let you know what you are looking at. The church captures breathtaking views of the city from a 360-viewing platform at the top of the spire looking down into colleges and Radcliffe Square to the far distance of Boars Hill. It's well worth the energy, effort and price for anyone visiting.

Chapter Twelve

CORNMARKET STREET

After all the hard work of reading and the travelling on this imagination tour of Oxford, a treat is thoroughly deserved. I have a treat that will beat a Wonka Bar: probably the best cookies I have ever had in my life reside in Oxford.

Established in 1983, the Ben's Cookies is no bigger than a nicely sized kitchen. It is small, quaint and tucked in the Covered Market. It can be found off the High Street at the top, near Carfax. There is another route from Cornmarket Street, opposite MacDonald's (I honestly dislike the fact that I've mentioned the fast-food joint, but it helps you find the place). It has an entrance that looks like a dead-end but it takes you through some shops that look like they are from the times of Shakespeare. Then, on the left, you find it continues to the Covered Market.

Ben's Cookies

The reason for the cookies being so fantastic is the secret, which I have tried to crack, of the melted chocolate in the centre of the cookie. It's not hot, it's a soft, velvet, chocolate goo that slips down to your stomach. I have travelled to probably 20 of the 50 states in the US, a country famous for its cookies, as well as large chunks of the globe and I am yet to come across anything like these, either in a store or homemade.

If chocolate does not grab you, there are a variety of flavours; fruit, peanut butter, coconut, ginger, and oatmeal and raisin. I have never tried these as I am hooked on the taste of a triple chocolate chip. Be warned though, the number of calories in these cookies means that one is more than enough!

The Covered Market

Once you've bought your cookie, there is an old market to discover. As the name suggests, this market is all undercover and the businesses are owned and run predominantly by local businesspeople. These shops have taken a hit lately due to the opening of the new mall called the Westgate Centre. However, this market has something more real and less fabricated than an industrial site. The market is officially 2 years older than the United States and designed by the architect of the Magdalen Bridge. The market contains pretty much anything and everything you could want. For food that has Oxford origins, there are Oxford sausages and sauces. There are Greek and Brazilian takeaways too. There are other food vendors selling vegetarian and traditional English meals that are cheap and portioned out in large quantities. If you look around, there are some quaint, hidden restaurants such as Georgina's or cafés such as Brown's.

Brown's looks like it would fit perfectly in an episode of the classic British comedy, *Only Fools and Horses*: simple, clean, English-style cooking, cracking for a full English, vegan or omnivore breakfast, and worth every penny. Georgina's restaurant/café is equally as tasty, with a more vintage feel, excellent sandwiches, and more vegetarian and vegan options. The ceiling is covered in cool posters from the many golden ages of cinema. There are also traditional butchers' shops in the market, some which have been there for over 100 years. Be aware of the hanging animals, which I'm sure are not for everyone. If shopping is on your mind, there are plenty of jewellery, kitchen equipment, coffee, clothing, shoe and watch stores to visit. We come to the end of the imagination tour but not to the end of the book. I have included details on other parts of Oxford that I'm sure will grab and amaze you.

Chapter Thirteen

OXFORD CASTLE

This castle has rumours of dating as far back as the Roman period but there is little to no evidence of that. The castle has taken on many forms and uses over the last 1000 years and has even been a part of some significant events in British history.

The castle still has some examples of it being part of Oxford's fortifications, but there is little left of that or the general defences of Oxford. If you want to have a good look at some of the city's old walls, you can find them in New College, near-perfectly preserved.

The castle was started after the Norman conquest by William the Conqueror around 1071 to 1073. We are not fully sure what it looked like, but we can guess from a castle that was built by Robert D'Oyly, the baron of Oxford at the time.

The first significant event for the castle and British history was in the 1140s. England had its first empress, Empress Matilda. Her father, King Henry I, had a son called Stephen. Stephen died at sea in 1120 and this left Matilda as the only direct heir to the throne. Matilda had married the Holy Roman Emperor, Henry V, and was based in Italy. Unfortunately for Matilda, he died in 1125 and together they had no children. In 1135, her father died and Matilda came back to claim the crown in 1139, but she faced opposition from the church and her cousin, Stephen, who had claimed the throne. In her attempt to take the throne back, she based herself in Oxford. However, the results of this civil war known as 'The Anarchy' caused Matilda to get trapped in Oxford Castle in the winter of 1142. Dressed in a white cloak, she scaled down the tower and escaped on foot across the frozen river and made her way to Abingdon. It would not be until 1153 that a full peace was organised. At this point, Matilda had a son that would be the successor to her cousin, Stephen. Matilda died in Rouen, France, in 1167. Her ghost is the most frequently seen in the castle, especially within the tower.

The castle then goes through several interesting phases. It would be owned by the monarchy, who then sold it to Francis James and Robert Younglove and was in turn sold to Christ Church. The college then leased the castle and grounds to local families. When the English Civil war broke out in 1642, royalists took over the city and improved the castle. At the end of the war, the castle walls were torn down.

Even with the walls down, the remaining parts of the castle still served a purpose and it was used as a prison. Whilst in prison, the prisoners would pay the wardens and guards for the lodgings. There were even hangings, and the last lady to be hanged was in 1766, yet the most interesting, and one of the last, was a lady called Mary Blandy. Mary Blandy was a well-respected, intelligent and articulate lady. In 1746 she fell for a Scotsman Captain, William Cranstoun. In 1751, the two intended to marry but it was revealed Cranstoun had already been married. The lovers went to Scotland to have the marriage annulled but it did not seem to be getting anywhere. Mary's father was unhappy with the marriage, and this would cost him his life. Mary was tried for the murder of her father in 1752. She claimed that she had given her father a love potion sent to her by Cranstoun. It turned out to be arsenic. She was found guilty and hanged just outside the prison. It is even claimed that her ghost can be seen on misty mornings around the castle complex, as she searches for her lover Cranstoun.

The prison stopped operating in 1996 and the council changed the site into a hotel in 2006. Cells were converted into guestrooms and rooms associated with capital and corporal punishment were converted into offices.

Chapter Fourteen

THREE OXFORD MUSEUMS

The Ashmolean, Pitt Rivers & Oxford University Museum

'Wonderful things, exquisitely displayed'
Bill Bryson

'To travel through the galleries is to be handed a round-the-world ticket on a tour of history'

The Times

W e talked earlier about the Museum of the History of Science, formally known as the Ashmolean. We should also spend some time talking about the New Ashmolean as well as the combined Oxford University Museum and Pitt Rivers Museum.

I have many fond memories of both museums from childhood. From visits with the school and having my first kiss and body squeezed by a girl, to seeing antiquities of ancient history, to the extinct animals somehow collected and preserved in the Natural History Museum.

The Ashmolean

Museum of Art and Archaeology

'He (Ashmole) did so because the knowledge of Nature is very necessary to human life and health'

Ashmolean Museum website.

The Ashmolean has an interesting history, starting off as a private collection of goods collected from around the world. It now shows a jigsaw of human history.

The original collection was not collected by
Elias Ashmole. They were collected by a man
called John Tradescant the Elder and his son
John Tradescant the Younger. It is a strange
tale as the original collection was from the
family Tradescant, yet the museum bears the
name Ashmolean, which was from the man
who bought the collection from Tradescant.
Tradescant was a well-travelled gardener who
had collected many items from across the
world, which, as it grew, became known as
'The Ark.' Tradescant and his wife Hester had
agreed to leave this to their son and during this

became acquainted with Ashmole. Ashmole had survived the civil war was on good terms with the King and had become acquainted with the Tradescant family. Unfortunately, Tradescant Jr died and the family decided to leave 'The Ark' to Ashmole. The relations between the two fell apart, especially when Tradescant Snr died, and Hester, due to several arguments, refused to give the goods over to Ashmole. Strangely, Hester died and was found lying face-first in a pond. Ashmole then bought the remnants of 'The Ark' and in 1675 the world's first museum was established. The first location for the museum is the new Science Museum on Broad Street, which still has an excellent collection of goods. The new museum is off St Giles and opposite the Randolph Hotel.

As you approach the building you can't help but feel the approaching history you are about to see from the world's first museum. The outside has a clearly Roman, Greek and

Oxford combined look to it. A white façade, with large Roman columns and Greek statues depicting scenes from ancient mythology, with the outside showing a clear theme of blending modern and ancient worlds, with modern art features being placed out front and revolving electric doors allowing entry into the museum. I took a brief look at Bill Bryson's book, *Notes on a Small Island,* and *The Road to Little Dribbling.* He clearly has a love of the museums in Oxford as they feature repeatedly, usually gushing with praise for the variety of the exhibitions and the addictiveness of the exhibits. He is not wrong. Over a million people per year agree by visiting the museum. All the great civilisations reside here. You enter and take note of the gallery to the left and to the right a staircase going both up and down. You head to the front desk, looking modern and sleek, with an ancient marble statue 5 times the size of a standard human as well as a plaque from the world's first civilisation: the Sumerians. Then, there is

a curious slogan on the side of the wall, stating 500,000 years of history. A friend of mine was with me and had a fascination with dinosaurs and human history. He pointed to the fact that modern humans have only been around since 150,000. My curiosity already engorged in entry to the Ashmolean caused me to query at the desk what they had that was human and from half a million years ago. I was asked to come back and all would be revealed later.

We delved inside, seeing the newly designed exhibitions containing a wealth of old material and goods collected from all over the world. From ancient Rome and Greece statues of forgotten heroes and gods, in the Japan section, there are Samurai swords and suits of armour, and from Egypt there are mummies and even part of a restored building. The Egyptian collection is the second largest predynastic collection in the world, second only to Cairo. It holds the greatest collection of Raphael drawings in the world. It is clear to see that the building houses an impressive collection from so many periods you can get happily lost inside. But getting lost is part of the joy here, as we quickly notice the museum has been designed to allow communication and links between cultures. 5th century Greece is just across the way from 5th century India, and 13th century Africa is near to 13th century China, allowing you to feel lost but see connections between civilisations is a unique feature that I've not seen in any other museum. When walking around we did, and it was only when coming full circle to the desk and the 500,000 years of history that we remembered what was promised. There was only the answer of 'we have pottery from 10,000 years ago, which is close enough.' Having not the heart and being British I did not point out the

difference between 10,000 and half a million.
I simply nodded and thanked the volunteers
for their help, then ascended to the roof cafe.
This café is well worth a visit, albeit you pay
a little extra for a decent coffee, but you
know that this will be going to the upkeep
of something special. Be sure to take in the
views from the outdoor section of the café,
with incredible views towards Boars Hill. The
thing that grabs me is what Bryson seems to
dislike and the Ashmolean has blended well.
They have separated the café from the rest
of the museum: keeping the shopping centre
feel out of the museum but enough to let you
bask in a good drink and hard walk around
a beautiful site.

Their collection also contained the last dodo
seen in Europe, which can now be found in
the Natural History Museum, supposedly
an inspiration to Charles Dodgson (Lewis
Carroll, author of *Alice in Wonderland.)*

Oxford University Museum of Natural History & The Pitt Rivers

The Museum of Natural History is a fascinating museum. The outside architecture grabs you immediately, as well as the giant Redwood tree to the left and the dinosaur footprints on the grass in front of the main  entrance. The prints were discovered in the North of Oxford and these were replicated outside the Natural History Museum. It's a lot of fun jumping from step to step, imagining you are hunting like a dinosaur. The museum houses a large array of dinosaurs and a significant number have come from Oxfordshire, including the Megalosaurus whose footprints can be seen outside, the Cetiosaurus, the Eastreptospondyies and the Cumneira. All these dinosaurs roamed our now peaceful valleys around 168 – 175 million years ago. In Oxfordshire in 1676, bones were discovered and given to the Ashmolean but the people working there could not have had a clue as to what they were and some even thought they were the bones of giant humans. This is the beginnings of the conflict of science versus religion, which was to come back to Oxford in the 1860s.

There are more modern and extinct wonders hidden in the museum. You enter through a relatively small entrance and up worn steps into a large, beautiful room, where you are confronted by whale bones and, in the centre of the room and in front of where you enter, you see a large replica of a Tyrannosaurus rex. With blackened bones and a replica head at its base. The room's interior reminds me of two places. Paddington Station combined with the Natural History Museum in London. Paddington Station and the Natural History Museum have wrought iron supports that flamboyantly reach their way to the top to support the roof, almost like tree branches. Red and sandstone brick make up the walls and the pillars were made by stonemasons using every type of stone in the British Isles. The rest of the room contains boxes of glass and wooden exhibits placed in broken rows. If you go towards the T-Rex and look to your left, you will see Charles Dodgson's dodo from *Alice in Wonderland,* or at least the remnants of the dodo: the head and part of the leg. It is also the last dodo to be seen alive in Europe. The reason there is not more of it left is that it was in such a decayed state in the 1770s that the curators of the museum decided to burn it. Luckily, someone removed the head and foot.

We also believe that Dodgson came to the museum to view the great debate that took place in the museum on 'The Theory of Evolution.' 7 months after Charles Darwin published his Theory of Evolution in 1859, a significant debate took place in the Natural History Museum. If you want to go to the room where the debate took place, you need to get special permission and go upstairs. It was between many people but mainly revolved around Thomas Henry Huxley and Bishop Samuel Wilberforce. Supposedly 700 to 1000 people attended and we know that Charles Dodgson had paid the museum a fee only the week before. During the debate, Wilberforce had supposedly questioned Huxley whether it was through his grandfather or his grandmother that he claimed his descent from a monkey. Supposedly, Huxley replied that he would not be ashamed to have a monkey for his ancestor, but he would be ashamed to be related to a man who used his great gifts to obscure the truth. Darwin did not attend because he was either ill or weary of life. This was, and is, still considered to be one of the great scientific events and debates of history and it would eventually become the event that cemented the common belief in the Theory of Evolution. If this does not grab you, nor the inspiration from being surrounded by statues of great scientists and philosophers, there is another museum with its entrance to the far-left corner. This is the Pitt Rivers Museum and it is a museum of anthropology, that's the study of you, me and other humans. It is filled with a bevvy of artefacts, including some shrunken heads. Good luck in finding them in the room, as it's almost a maze of exhibits. They come from all over the world, and the aim is to show the different ways humans live.

Chapter Fifteen

CHRIST CHURCH

Welcome to Christ Church, almost 500 years old and its grounds in the city centre span over 175 acres at the time of writing this. A college of sandstone, with grand architecture and associated with some of the most significant people and events in British history. The college has influenced and been a part of

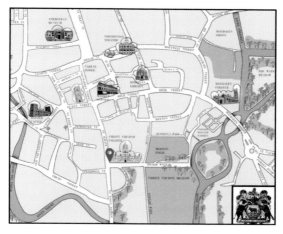

many key events in Oxford and British history. With connections to kings and prime ministers, Wonderlands, wizards, some of the greatest minds in human history, and even lays claim to be the place where the first-ever British hot-air balloon was launched.

The grounds of the college started with a priory, which was built around the burial of the patron saint of Oxford and the university. The priory of St Frideswide was built on a nunnery in 1122 and this links to the foundations of Oxford. You can still see parts of these buildings in the Christ Church Cathedral, which was built between 1160–1120. It is the only cathedral in Oxford and one of the smallest in England. Saint Frideswide is the patron saint of Oxford and Oxford University. She is believed to have existed in the 8th century and has a couple of interesting tales. She has a variety of accounts of her being chased by a king, who, unable to gain her attention, either breaks his neck or becomes blind. Either way, she survives and establishes a priory until her death around 727AD.

The college doesn't come into being until the 1530s with Henry VIII taking charge of the grounds and renaming the grounds Christ Church. The changing of this was a part of Henry VIII's greater plans for the country, which included changing the country's Christian religion being led by the Pope to it being led by the British monarchy.

The monarchy and parliament would return to Christ College during the reign of Charles I in 1642. An argument had broken out between Charles I and parliament, causing Charles I to leave London and set up a government in Oxford. Charles took up residence in Christ Church inside the Deanery and he created his parliament inside the Great Hall. King Charles took up residence for 4 years, lost Oxford to parliamentarians on several occasions and eventually lost his head in London in 1649.

Alice in Wonderland

Into the more recent era, where we get into wonderlands and wizards. There is plenty to see related to *Alice in Wonderland* both in the city and in Christ Church. Lewis Carroll was the pen name for Charles Lutwidge Dodgson. He was an excellent mathematician, gained a double-first during his studies and became a tutor for the College, where he taught for over

30 years. A lot more detail will be discussed about Dodgson in chapter sixteen. This is where Dodgson met Alice who, along with the College, would become his inspiration for the story of *Alice in Wonderland*. Alice was the daughter of the dean and they stumbled upon Dodgson whilst he was photographing the cathedral.

The family struck up a friendship and Dodgson took members of the family on boat trips where he would tell tales of the adventures of *Alice in Wonderland*. Some of the influences for the book are based inside the cathedral and the surrounding parts of the campus.

The Cheshire Cat tree is claimed by several locations around the country. Even though it is associated with the Christ Church there is little evidence, and the verger of the cathedral, Jim Godfrey, has also denied this. However, there is in the Pococke Garden the tree that inspired the Jabberwocky but gaining entry does require permission from the college.

There are plenty of other things to see related to Dodgson. If you go to the cathedral you can see Alice's image in one of the stained-glass windows. You will need to go halfway down the hall and look above the fireplace. You can also find Henry Liddell, Alice Liddell's father, who is buried in the cathedral.

Interestingly, Alice did find romance in the college. She fell for Queen Victoria's son, Leopold, whilst he studied at the college. Their romance was stopped from going further by Queen Victoria who didn't want Leopold marrying a commoner. They both went on to marry and interestingly they both had children. Alice Liddell had a son who was named Leopold and Leopold had a daughter who was named Alice.

Harry Potter

If you are more into a modern children's tale, then look no further than *Harry Potter*. The Great Hall was meant to originally be the filming location for the dining hall scenes, but the Hall could not fit in four tables for the four houses, so a set replicating Christ Church's Hall was built in London instead. You can visit the set in Harry Potter Studio Tours in Watford. If you are looking for actual film locations you can visit the steps that lead into the great hall, which were featured in *The Philosophers Stone* and *The Chamber of Secrets*.

If you fancy some live-action Harry Potter without the flying, you can go see Quidditch being played by the colleges. They even have a league. The Christ Church team trains on Wednesday and Saturday afternoons at University Parks.

If you are looking for some souvenirs, you can visit Broad Street, where you will find the Shop of Secrets, or you could visit Christ Church gift shop. Both are full of Harry Potter merchandise.

AUTHORS OF OXFORD

I intend to expand on this section in another book, as there have been so many authors in Oxford for both fiction and non-fiction that it seems unfair to try to squeeze this into this book. I've included these three simply because I have knowledge of them and their works. There is so much more to discuss. Geoffrey of Monmouth, Sir Phillip Pullman, Dr. Johnson, Richard Dawkins, Stephen Hawking, John Betjeman, Kenneth Grahame, Vera Brittain, Terry Jones, Jonathan Swift, Percy Shelly, Phillip Larkin, Thomas Eliot, Dr Seuss, Robert Burton, Colin Dexter, Oscar Wilde, Agatha Christie and Christopher Hitchens.

I have limited this to their adventures and related locations in the city centre of Oxford:

1. Charles Dodgson
2. C. S. Lewis
3. J. R. R. Tolkien

Chapter Sixteen

ALICE LIDDELL & CHARLES DODGSON

There are so many interesting locations to visit related to Alice and Dodgson. I have already touched upon how the two met and their relationship within Christ Church in chapter fourteen.

The real Alice was born in 1852 and lived until 1934. The day and date are according to the Mad Hatter. When Alice and Hatter met is the day and date of Alice Liddell's birth. Alice was one of three sisters and her father, Henry Liddell, the Dean of Christ Church. The family soon became friends, with Dodgson particularly becoming friends with the Dean's wife Lorina and the three sisters Lorina, Edith, and Alice Liddell. Dodgson soon started taking pictures of the girls and taking them out into Oxford and on boating trips from Folly Bridge. On the 4th of July 1862 on one of the regular boating trips, Dodgson told the tale of Alice in Wonderland. Alice was so smitten with the story that she demanded Dodgson write it down. It was finally completed in November 1864 and was known as *Alice's Adventures Under Ground,* published in 1865 with the new name *Alice's Adventures in Wonderland.* Oxford now celebrates Alice and her adventures every year on the 4th of July.

Alice Liddell's father was the Dean of Christ Church and Dodgson had a frosty relationship with him. Both lived at opposite ends of Christ Church. Dodgson's last lodgings were to the left of the gate as you enter Tom's Quad. The Deanery was on the opposite side near the entrance to Peckwater Quad. This relationship with the family came to an end on June 1863, with Mrs Liddell stating that her daughters were not to be left alone with Dodgson and in later years he was not invited to Alice's wedding. Dodgson continued with his work, and in 1871 produced *Through the Looking Glass.*

Alice's Tour

For this self-contained mini tour, you would best start at Magdalen Bridge and walk towards the city centre and Carfax Tower along the High Street. When you start this tour, you will find that High Street takes you towards the Red Queen's and Mad Hatter's establishments.

"All Oxford called him The Mad Hatter. He would stand at the door of his furniture shop . . . always with a top-hat at the back of his head, which, with a well-developed nose and a somewhat receding chin, made him an easy target for the caricaturist," wrote the Reverend W. Gordon Baillie in a letter to *The Times* of March 19, 1931.

On the right-hand side of the road is the Hatter's place of work, 22 High Street. The Hatter's real name was Thomas Randall, who preferred to be called Hatter. He was a tailor and Hatter to Dodgson as well as locals and students. He was even elected as Mayor of Oxford in 1859 and seems to have lasted 2 years at the job.

As you continue up the High Street, on the left-hand side is the Old Bank Hotel, which was a bank in Dodgson's time, and we have the ledgers from his banking days that show he paid £5 to a person by the name of 'Hatter.' Today this would be £150.

You will see the Mitre Pub on the right, which is currently closed for refurbishment at the time of writing this and will reopen in January 2021. Don't worry, it is a listed building so the changes should be minimal to the pub. The connection to Alice in Wonderland is through Mary Pickett, who was the governess to the Liddell girls, and she became associated with the Red Queen. She generally escorted the girls and went on several boating trips with the girls and Dodgson until she married in 1870 and ran the Mitre Pub for 50 years!

As you come to Carfax Tower, take a left and down St Aldates towards Christ Church. On the left make sure to stop at the Museum of Oxford, also known as the Oxford Town hall. It contains all sorts of Alice and Dodgson artefacts, including photos and memorabilia associated with the tales of *Alice in Wonderland*. A little further on you will find an entrance to Christ Church If you want to learn about Alice's adventures and inspirations in the college, please check out chapter fourteen. In the college, you will find the Jabberwocky tree, Liddell's and Dodgson's residence, a stain-glass Alice and the not-Cheshire Cat tree.

Opposite Christ Church and across St. Aldates you will find Alice's shop and Café Loco. Both feature prominently in Alice's life as they were both shops during her time at Christ Church and she visited both. Café Loco is linked to both Morse and *Alice in Wonderland*, with Alice and Dodgson having visited the café 150 years ago. The café now hosts prints of John Tenniel's work, the original artist for *Alice in Wonderland,* as well as photos from the filming of Lewis (a spinoff to Morse) at the café.

'Well, this is the very queerest shop I ever saw!' Chapter 5, *Through the Looking Glass* by Lewis Carroll

Alice's Shop, 150 years ago, served Alice sweets. Today, it sells all kinds of trinkets associated with her adventures. It features in *Through the Looking Glass*. The story tells of Alice entering the old sheep shop, which is run by a sheep- apparently reflecting the bleating voice of the actual lady who ran the shop. Alice's entry into the shop is one full of curiosity as anything she looks at on the shelves floats away, and eventually leads to Alice leaving the shop to go on a boat ride with the sheep. The boat ride is meant to reflect how the shop would frequently flood and the owners had to use a boat to get around.

Head a little further down the road and you will come to a pub and a bridge called The Folly. The trip Dodgson, his friend, and the three Liddell sisters took on July 4th, 1862, was from here to Binsey and Godstow. You can hire a punt from here with the company Steamers and, if you are feeling particularly adventurous, you could take the boat or punt up to The Perch pub in Binsey, where Lewis Carroll made his first public reading of *Alice in Wonderland*.

Chapter Seventeen

THE INKLINGS WITH C. S. LEWIS & TOLKIEN

An Irishman and a South African come to Oxford and the two came together to produce arguably two of the most famous epics ever written. *Lord of the Rings*, *The Hobbit* and *The Tales of Narnia* have all been world hits as books and movies, and Oxford has a part to play in these tales.

How they came together

They both ventured into Oxford; Tolkien as a student at Exeter College in 1911 and Lewis as a student in 1916 at University College. Both men enlisted and fought in World War I, and both were affected by the horrors they experienced, which was reflected in their writing. You can really see this in Frodo and Sam's reactions to war at the end of the *Lord of the Rings*. Interestingly they both fought in the Battle of the Somme. They returned to Oxford University and were in the English Faculty. However, they did not meet until 11th May 1926 at a Merton College English Faculty Tea. C.S. Lewis remarked of Tolkien on their first meeting, *"No harm in him: only needs a smack or so."*

This might have had something to do with their religious views. Tolkien was a keen Catholic and C.S. Lewis was an atheist. Both men soon began to connect over their love of literature. They both had an interest in Norse mythology and met regularly in Lewis' room in Magdalen Colleges. Tolkien, with his love of languages, had translated the story of *Beowulf*, as well as other Norse and British mythology. Quickly they became friends and would exchange notes and details on their works as well as theology. The Norse mythology was of such interest that a group was formed, and others were invited to join. They began to meet to read the myths and discuss them, meeting once a week on a Thursday. This group was known as the Coalbiters. The word relates to the telling of noble adventures and sagas around the roaring hearth (Coalbiters were those who lounged so close to the fire in winter that they might as well be biting the coal.) By the late 1920s, the group meetings began to end and new life in the Inklings began to form. This group expanded and included as many as 25 people including regulars, irregulars and guests. They met at a variety of locations across Oxford, including Magdalen College, the East Gate Hotel, the Kings Arms, the White Horse Pub, The Trout and the Eagle and Child. The Eagle and Child, known as the 'Bird and Baby' to the group, is the more famous location associated with the Inklings. There is even a corner in the Eagle in Child today dedicated to the Inklings and shows the spot where they sat and discussed literature on a Tuesday morning. The East Gate Hotel is opposite Magdalen College and has an area dedicated to the Inklings where you can also sit and drink. During this time, Tolkien and Lewis began to have discussions on religion and eventually Lewis converted back to Christianity and in part, this was the inspiration for a significant amount of work for *Narnia*, with Aslan the lion, who has aspects of Jesus' life, including the resurrection.

They both drew from their experience of World War I and II. Narnia has the children come and stay with a writer during World War II, which is what happened to Lewis whilst he lived in Oxford. Tolkien refuted the idea that his books were associated with World War II, however, the psychological effects of Sam and Frodo from having been in war seem to reflect this. Things were never the same again for Frodo and Sam, with Sam finally plucking up the courage to talk to and marry Rosie (Rose Cotton.)

One other common theme is the trees. It is said that the tree that inspired Tree Beard in *Lord of the Rings* was in the Botanical Gardens opposite Magdalen College. Both authors at the end of *Narnia* and after the battle of Helm's Deep had the trees come to life to help rescue the heroes.

The Inklings Tour

To start your tour, I recommend the best place to begin is Magdalen College. You have the deer park and Addison's walk, where both Tolkien and Lewis would walk and debate theology and discuss their books. It also contains C. S. Lewis' room, contained in the New Building. Lewis' office can be found at Staircase 3, Room 3.

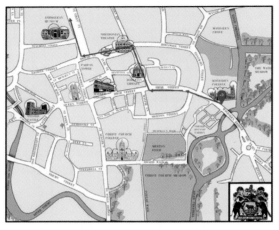

Across from Magdalen College, you will find
The Botanic Garden that use to contain Tree
Beard and was unfortunately cut down in 2014.

As you head west, up the High Street, you can stop at the East Gate Hotel where the Inklings would meet.

Further up, you will see St Mary's Church. If you go down the most western passage of the church, you will see two fawns, a door with a lion and a lamp post. All the inspirations for a tale of *Narnia*.

Beyond this is Radcliffe Camera which is said to be the inspiration for the Morgoth Spire, a castle of Sauron in *Lord of the Rings.*

Continue north and you will find the Kings Arms, another pub for Inklings meetings.

West again, and you will find the White Horse Pub, famous for many things and another meeting location of the Inklings.

The final stop of the Inklings tour is west of the White Horse at the Bird and Baby, also known as the Eagle and Child. This is where C. S. Lewis first handed out the proofs for *The Lion the Witch and the Wardrobe*. It also has a dedicated corner to the Inklings and their meetings.

GOODBYE

I always put this quote into my travel books and hope it inspires you to go and visit these places:

"while it's tempting to play it safe, the more we're willing to risk, the more alive we are. In the end, what we regret most are the chances we never took. And I hope that explains, at least a little, this journey on which I am about to embark."

Frasier: May 13, 2004

As you can see, Oxford is a wonderful place and having put this book together, I realised how much was there, how much I had not seen and how much needed to be shown to those coming into this city or are thinking about visiting.

One thing I would recommend, and is one of my travel rules: don't try to cram it all in and run around the city trying to see everything.

It simply won't work. It has the potential to stress you out and damage your trip or holiday.

Pick the things you want to see the most and check them out.

If you'd like to know even more about my travels and this city, follow me on my blog:

https://welcomeworldwalker.com/

You can also contact me about personal tours.

This is not the end though. I have attached an Oxford Crossword with some obvious and some cryptic clues, enjoy!

Thank you for joining me on this journey.

Oxford Crossword

Across

1. A traveller's tale involving giants and little men
2. A musical skull
3. The importance of being wild
4. Bilbo would never be the same
5. A wonderful Wagner character created to inspect
6. The richest college in Oxford
7. A theory was debated in an Oxford Museum
8. A traveller and python

Down

1. Renamed under Henry VIII and the residence of the Jabberwocky tree.
2. A Brief History of Time
3. Green eggs and ham please.
4. Whatever happened to the cat in the box?
5. You'll need this to fight bacteria
6. Dr Johnson I presume?
7. Frankenstein's husband
8. A bit of Stephen Fry and ....

OTHER BOOKS BY THIS AUTHOR

Where should I stay in Sicily?

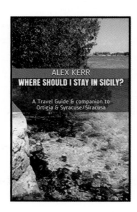

RECOMMENDED PLACES TO VISIT IN OXFORD

Oxford Visitor Information Centre

Address: 15-16 Broad St, Oxford OX1 3AS
Monday to Saturday 9:30am to 5:30 pm
Sunday 0:30 am to 4:30 pm

Many thanks to all those who have supported me:

Gran, Dad, Jason & Laura.

Marthe Mostervik x

Julia-Carolin Zeng with Charlie

Debra Kingsman